A COMMON WORLD

Andrew Mossin

The Bodily Press
Amherst, MA

A Common World

Copyright © 2025 Andrew Mossin

All rights reserved. Except for brief passages quoted for usage in online or print sources (e.g. newspaper, magazine, podcast), no part of this book may be reproduced in any form or by any means, electronic or mechanical, including photocopying and recording, or by any information storage and retrieval system, without permission in writing from the publisher.

This book is set in Garamond Premier Pro.
Book design and layout by Eliot Cardinaux.
eliotcardinaux.com

Cover artwork by Arthur Wesley Dow
August Moon, 1905
Five color wood block print on heavy cream Japanese paper
4 1/2 x 7 in. (11.43 x 17.78 cm.)

Bodily Press logo designed by Katya Popova.
popova.space

A COMMON WORLD

Also by Andrew Mossin

Poetry & Chapbooks

Drafts for Shelley
From Blake's Notebook
The Epochal Body
The Veil
Exile's Recital
Torture Papers
Stanzas for the Preparation of Perception
The Fire Cycle
North & East: Daybooks
Black Trees
Whitman at the Bardo

Memoir

A Son from the Mountains

Criticism

Male Subjectivity and Poetic Form in "New American" Poetry
Thinking with the Poem: Essays on the Poetry and Poetics of Rachel Blau DuPlessis

Rather than discovering or telling about the world, it is a matter of producing an equivalent, which would be the Book, in which everything would be said, without anything's being reported.

> Édouard Glissant

The common day and night—the common earth and waters.

> Walt Whitman

In memory of Gustaf Sobin
1935-2005

&

For Rachel Blau DuPlessis

Table Of Contents

I: Rites of Observation

A Common World	13
The New Spirit	20
Parallel Suites for the Re-Recognition of Innate Form	26
Convergences	38
Attunement	45

II: Collecting the Signs

The Separation of Earthly Objects	53
Autobiography of Spirit: Novitiate Series	66
Field Notes from a Light Storm	72
Four Georgics	79
Earth Light, Earth Sound	85

III: Sentences from a Sensual Earth

Mourning: A Work Song	93
Late River Song	105
Nocturnal Suite	116
Convergences (New Series)	123
The Virtual Son	132
Notes & Acknowledgements	145

I: Rites of Observation

And it is all one to me
Where I am to begin; for I shall return there again.
Parmenides (tr. David Gallop)

A Common World

> The common world is what we enter when we are born and what we leave behind when we die. It transcends our lifespan into past and future alike; it was there before we came and will outlast our brief sojourn in it.
> Hannah Arendt

1

The house where skin is, coronal leaves, citrus
under the tongue. The purple region of bruise

like lightness to the touch, a hand that reaches
beneath one's clothing at 4 in the afternoon

to refinish the act, remake some solidity where
once a curtain was developed. Not sprung

but weighted, not calendric but serpentine, as
leaves are litmus tests of our ability to crave joy.

We move as one animal moves, the region of
likeness to another is this mantic space

we endure and re-associate with kinship. A sky
where there once was ceiling. We say it's

laughter purpling the room. Your gaze lifted to
find us nightly. It's symmetrical yet pulled

apart, so the terrain lessens pain. We come back
to make these things mean something

newer, less viable to the touch, yet resonant
as paper forces us yet again to embark

on a journey. Words come back, the delicacy of
witness, that oneself isn't enough to survive.

Under water. At sea. The names are restless to
come by. Hermes walks past. A day inside

his eyes and I'm moving forward again, without effort
or care. The streets have become familiar

against all odds. What can anyone say but
how long and for what purpose?

2

I'm coming into it, the patterns that re-work
sound, séance of the stilled night. A habit

that seeks company. When I'm sitting here with
you, the realism is complete. Your eyes

objective, willful, abject—all at the same instant
of remove. What I was saying—fond left-over

words, the realities they portended, you said
it wasn't enough to undo beginnings, we had

little else left but its companion skill: theft. What
I said we said again. Replacement's rejoinder.

The pluralism of voice that is both invocation
and revocation. A seam down the middle where light

offers a gift for strangers. An alphabet cut
from the wood of a cypress. Stranded

daylight. Ripostes of shadow. Askance. Shoulder to
shoulder. Your name little more than a pattern I

come close to. Now and again to say it
here in the eventual fold of after-thinking:

in another nest the master of the maze
stilled, cordoned off, the regional inflection

as West Virginia nights come back, heavy
with cottonwood and cicada wings, moth

sweet nights that I'm no longer part of
but re-possess, as if articles could be sent

ahead, carrying fortunes, small objects
from another lifetime.

3

And if everything becomes made less sure?
The weight of language, lately I've come to resume its

intricacies. My father sits where he always
sat, the days are thicker with his intentions

years after his death, even as I'm less available to
hear him out. His eyes move with my own.

Blond wood is shelf wood. One is carrying
the beginnings of a cabinet or bookshelf

in mind. So that the room can deepen.
Night light can withstand the open door.

A way of entering, as if ghostly marks
awaited you. And it's something like

shelter, the sky opening above the room
inside a circle of light, the way river sounds

complete decades of audition, prehensile
reminders of where one's been. Here in the

nest, in the rapid waters of nesting, purple
light, skin bearing the odor of tobacco, as if you

were the light, skin was its sister, shining apart
from the table where lines were drawn

opposites in all directions.

4

Reading for what is coming, the delay in
transition, one is always alone in the

daytime, to keep alive where light is
coming, to see it open again, you can't say

the house is here and not here, but another
word spaces things out, you see the words

spaced out between phases, time situates
the body, you come to it, older than you were

to stare at its pieces, the lament is not realism
but a kind of forthcoming gesture. Human

hands you say meant to do human things.
Acts and speech. The common thread breaking as

if dawn were closure on the banks of the river.

5

It's not one but two. Vacancy is not
the point. You are hearing another in the

last place you expected. The river is
reddening in the dusk. What one does is

never less than what one wants not
to have done. Perched above the river

we were kids dancing inside skin.
Your hand was motherless as soft linen.

I carried one piece to the edge and watched
it drop. The sunlight steady in the room

where the bridge is moving left to right
in mind's eye. Right to left. A canopy has

opened, lifts us back from the water's edge.
What did you mean to tell us, but felt

reversed in yourself? A landscape is
nothing more or less than one's hand

moved into the light, taken back.

6

We are coming to the last most
seen things, the most last seen things

of a world. Devoid of sensation and
imbued with its radiant spell

the days limited and short, we are companion
with the light in our eyes, the river you

are moving toward can open your eyes,
as you settle in mud and callow lilies.

From the west you say the reach of
Colorado water is gone, the river has

vanished along the fire line, each
disappears from view, the landscape

fading out as one runs parallel to
light that crosses the desert floor as exact

phases of sun that is crossing the
earth as it vanishes from view.

Our entire body was warm to the touch
when it entered the current. Your

name perjured how many times over. Skin
is innocent of what it can't recall.

Loose clothing, wear it to the river dance.
Jump into September's last song. Light is mysterious.

Go inside its means. Travel its branch.
Opaque dusk, chapel salt. The earth that is

worn smooth again, canyon and river light in situ.
Smother their inner still point. Gift its dusk

out again, farther than touch.

12 September 2020

THE NEW SPIRIT
   For Nathaniel Mackey

    Don't we rise in fact downward?
        César Vallejo, *Trilce* (tr. Clayton Eshleman)

1

From the first it was water, a language of collective
mediation. We saw the late seas spread their oars

amid bird color, the buffed delay of daylight's reflection.
Abandoned at first, we'd made our way back to basics

in plural telling of the same journey, so we could grow
older inside its skin, kettle drum darkness

that became darker than lotus plant in spring, I could
cut its blessing in half, and come back to wander the way one

moves over the earth in pieces, low waters of savannahs I
was dreaming to resurrect, thoughtscape's dimension

recombined, the plantain fruit slipped from my left palm,
bird-starved, littoral movement, the way each of us

changes direction toward holiness to recognize partitions
between the where-to-be and where-to-become, wordless

as sky is heavenless, the board filled with painted arrows
that lead upward, through the days without color or actuality.

Here is one piece, now another, drawn in haste, a window
overlooking November's last dry days. I'm without tribunal

or resting spot, just this one roof to watch over,
this codex that expands, loosens with every day, so that the hands

make place for its pages even as the light at sunrise
suggests a world less made than undergone. There's little

intervention, the days marked by their patterns, flowing
unflowing, cautionary tales I'm gathering like so many red signs

painted above the Atlantic. You can slide your body into
each crease, dried slip of the hand become tripped up

by revenant light. So there can be no distinction
between foreground and background, the weight is equally

worn through each sitting, another's hand processing
the changes. Here's regret balanced with ardor, a woman's

mouth you once drew as a child, blacker than your hair, darker
than sunlight inside your left palm. You slide into its

contours the way color is a movement distilled,
broader than the ocean's blade.

2

To go off script, tell the tale straight, tell it without inversion
or pause to stop in place, gather your thoughts. Inside

was outside, the bright sun had come into it again, the script
was stolen, forged, we'd seen it before, in the time it took

to read the light you could see its passing. In that time craving so many
waters, the weight of design laid by currents, you said it's

the form of our making, creased, recalcitrant, a
collect of language, profit-free, prophetless, inside these

fugitive phrases, stalled and meeting you at the doorway. Was there one
awaiting rescue or another written out? Who's going to notice

their absence, the way light is drawn across a sunlit room in July
but comes from inside the room not outside. Identity's simpler to police

when the act is itself a warrant, spelled out here, in ground cover,
the locality of speech that's rising in the back of our

throats. As if cadence and cadenza brought themselves in line and
became our right to do this labor all over again, on this

surface, the oblong table that's littered with books and artifacts
of another's efforts. You can lay them out ten times over, converse

with sparrows at evening, cool throated thorax, pale skies
filled with their song, speech like a tablet of script unfolding

making itself known in this deictic form, this
parallel to oneself that travels outside again, ensues

where the tale breaks off, loosens in the hand, paper lengths
of line raveled and distorted in the bright noon sun.

3

A sliver of talk. Oneiric soft skull found in the woods.

Breaking old habits to remake the landscape as interior
vision. 'Notice how it fades,' one said. 'Let it become

song's lasting inquiry,' another offered. Back of both
the relapse into memory cycles, this zone of assonance

and co-creative talk. Moon cycle became fire cycle.
Hands on one's shoulder turned to re-define the torso

of one's lover. Skin and eyes. There was this colloquy of inadvertent
learning, the way we stored memory to repeat its legacy.

Paradise birds. Island summer inside candied light.
One's coming to tell the story backwards, learn

messages that mess with trust, turn the tables on loss so you
are with them in the book, trust and loss, inside and outside

like a bridge of wedged river rock, one makes the
daylight go back into its lair, one sits apart, daylong struggle just to

hear the light right, to get it down in one sentence. That
myth of perfection, some semblance of objective

clarity: like a message from one's internal companion
writing it all out on black unlined paper, the notebook

I'm learning to carry, steal away, as our narratives of daily life move
into the interior. Logic of the long day is this many minutes

collected into its pages. One watches some things on the ground
to hear them moving through a long slice of time.

Mornings start with its message, another's call, writing from
inside their destroyed works, left for no one to teach

or catch word of: 'This way to the birds' descent
fly up by red kindled stones,' as one marked daylight

with observation to catch it nailed to a board
in winter. The exigency of thought's last word, dream's

scorched horn sound, playing its tune off key, in lone
gestures becomes the sound it wasn't known for but held

otherwise, here on paper, the somatic sometime circle re-drawn
on black paper, board, wire, attached to a wing from a

hawk flying southwest.

4

Inhabit the late work, you said, open up the darkly grooved late
work. An *ars poetica* late in the day. No one waiting for it

to return, the work of it ongoing with reports of those leaving
the world, the daily toll. Language's futile last act to make some

bargain with their passing. To break down where the dying
aren't able to hear. World hurt where the days pass without notice.

Days without notice passing. The emptying out of words that
were heartless from the start. Without heart the eye loses track

to see its way through. A bit of heaven above. Not to lose heart
but losing the words for it. Soul abandoned by the body.

Bodies abandoned by souls. One is making way through the
late days, late work to read back what's written again, down the back

channel the water from a river cycle flowing back into the world.
Wordless at the end, without words for it, cessation's crib dawn

like light spread across the heavens, someone said, like a crown
of feathers brought into the world all over again.

Wind worked against us as we left them behind us, sometimes
hearing one call, blank face, the ending like a sojourn in emptied

out time. The house emptied out, then full again with their
presence. Inhabit the late work you said it would become a route

of congress, a passage into one's unspoken self. Here in the ending
we read of it again, the nocturnal suite that appends this text

and becomes a ritual brokered by bird light, the query of boats
passing at a distance, river language where there is no water for us

to set sail on. Someone waiting to pry open the pages
left unturned. You could say the elements were

shakier, hands moving into plum yellow light
as if to see the world again were to imitate thread, earth

light that was shifting inside beige walls of a room. Not
to lift but hear its rosewood flute, dream of the Bedouin

night we lay closer to, then fell back from. 'Daylight
is a system of falling,' one said. 'Here is the curled language

of it all over again,' another offered. Pale light, system
of its falling, curled light, sentences that lift up from their

origins to move, paratactically, across river skies. No one's
returning, the elements are fixed by what they can't reveal.

Visitation's common tropic, visible as any heaven.

23 December 2020

Parallel Suites for the Re-Recognition of Innate Form

> And now I ask myself,
> if no one entered the next room,
> who so carefully closed the door?
>   Xavier Villaurrutia, *Nostalgia for Death* (tr. Eliot Weinberger)

1

There is no birdsong where I am living, but the
elements have begun to move anew. One recovers

notes left under stones, the church that is always
open until 4 p.m. welcoming its strangers, as once

upon a time the end words were litmus, dust shells
bits of mollusk shell stuck to one's fingers.

We are how many decades apart from remnants
of ourselves, omnivorous words that become storehouses

of unsaid meaning, as if in transpiration the body had
found an empty site near the river's edge, walked

all morning to find it, moving into its currents for
the seventh time to find oneself again merely

absent, virtual as any creature of water.

2

Eternity lies elsewhere, we inhabit this ground
separated from those we once knew. The changing

light signifies a bodily transformation, as color
shifts against planes of experience, the earthly mud

captive as a tongue of barley, sweet grass run
through a random traveler's hand. 'We are not

of this world but contained by it,' we heard ourselves
repeat, monadic, effortful, as if we too were wood-like

creatures, spaced out along a landscape of improbable
darkness. We remembered a vineyard, the absence

of rain for twenty-three summers, the inseparableness of
mother tongue from fatherless eye. We twisted

awake inside a culvert of willow and ailanthus
leaves mixed with sweet wine. How did we understand that

orphaning was a quest, a dream of sovereignty? Or did we
divide the beginning from the middle, retelling our narrative

from inside the cutter's wheel?

3

In the prayer hall the Orphan rises alone...

There was this ludic introit, this occurrence
of paper and wind, an amending of one's place.

Scene by scene, we were standing shoulder to
shoulder with those who had abandoned us.

As dark earth, the summer slant of rain, processual
belief subsides. We lay down on the banks of the

Delaware, we huddled inside a tent close to the waters of
the Vistula, unable to distinguish between one

or another body of water, planes of existence shifted to
release us back to earlier orders. All we wish is

to stay, we said, where we have been kept, as bread
is given us and the work of it becomes symbolic, legible

as a script undertaken daily to receive what's been
stolen from us. A body comes forward to engage

us in conversation, another disappears into the side
of a building outside Athens. The wafers passed to us

when we were first believers have gone. Only the whiteness of
the moon inside a shelter above the city, glowing

in the vacated light of summer. The work of it is
triadic, insolvent, part and parcel of a landscape that

rests between tributary and tidal basin, the wash of
water moving one way, then another, slowly

immersing us in shadow.

4

'Who has transported us here into this darkness?'

Gnostic parallelisms accomplish our days. The yearning
for exaction coupled with errancy and false starts. One is standing

where we once were, the rites of passage new to them as
we are saying seven times seven, the years like vessels

we are traveling in. Words come to us from forty years ago,
the instructions oblique, reliquary, hardly worthy of

notice. We're signifying selves cut off from light, our habits
more difficult to trace, as one moves across a desert floor

a little after dawn to rest near an empty road, passing
no one, hearing only the stillness of the mesa dawn rising.

As we come back to the Mayan Book of Dawn to read of
their encampment, each tribe sleeping, returning to the

world of stones and light, the rhythm of their fracture
signified by stalwart watching for the star, to transform

their days. To become daylight, this sign of the dawn
passed among them, as they came away from the east

and stood shoulder to shoulder, passing the Great Hollow
moving eastward to arrive at the summit of Place of Advice

and find their names amongst each other, to name who they
had become, how they would be called.

5

It's never easy, the duty, diurnal, to record who
we were, then to leave one to the side of us, one

inside the other, mnemonic visitant, playbook's irritant who
lives as anything lives, insolvent, insurrectional, captive

and insistent as a corona of wet leaves, spaced
between the hands of a stranger. There is no one coming

to rescue the body, there is now and again the appeal
of another, resting on the floor with us, until light and shade

exact their offerings from us, white chalk placed in
the hands of a child, nearer than she was to us inside

this habitat, our sister, mourning the death of her
brother, weighted piecemeal narrative of initial separation.

One hears the voice of their deeper angel. One makes amends
while the ancient city sleeps, we can't thread our way

back or revisit the temple where once we lay down
in the blazing sun of late afternoon and cried out for you.

When I sat down I was sitting next to nothing I
could remember. His embrace…her face…

Their restricted movements, as if I'd become absent
from their position, weeks, then months, to record

their severance again. We are moving as the figure of
Sophia moves, with her faith broken, staggering

into view, consumed by earthly loss, exiled at
the edge of an encampment, her body

situated between earth and heaven. And what did
we imagine or invent to comfort her voice

when ours had become weakened from travel? We're awaking
to Sophia's voice again and again, stammering

her verses into the light.

6

There is hope in each portion, a thread we're re-working
to enunciate divinity or elaborate on a process that

reveals its Soul. Where we lay down was where we
began to see images from before, lateral scratches

down the arms of our mother and father, we had insinuated
faith where they fled from civil war, as once

we'd sat down on the dusty soil of Liknon and tasted
sorghum and salt, mined from fresh cut earth, quorum

of earth and sand, our feet resting just above a landing
of balsa wood. We got up, sang to them in Greek, sang

to them in Hebrew or Arabic, a song of shelter we said was
brewing, the earth sickness we had read of continued

inside each of us, as one by one we drew our breath over
empty glass. Skin was imperiled, the insides of our

body muted, transported, so that we saw the world as
illicit matter, as irremediable congress, seventh of

seven days we passed away from one object to another
as if encounter were prepositional, fate a factor

of one, then three, the supplication offered, steadily
across the months, to validate some stream of understanding

agnostic, parallel, enclosed by light.

7

So we could embrace the field and settle inside it
at the same time. No quarter given. Trees

rocked under a full moon, the side of buildings
saturated, rung through and through. I was waiting

for signal to come, when the signal came I passed
among the last of our days with gnostic prayer, errant

layer of water that cooled my skin, passing here and
there among blades of summer light, soaked through

as a hand is made to travel great distances....I
gave you sign of my return, you said there is no

reason to return, the waters will keep you safe. Each turn
an octave lower, we spelled our name on rags in blue

ink rescued from another era, we took collections to
find our passage out. A letter arrived from a friend, no

words written on the page, we stared at the empty
pages, one after the other, as spring passed

to summer, silence just before the solstice. The pages
folded, returning nightly, a signature without name

inside a codex of pond water.

8

Spirit is a purified act, as the materiality of our
purpose haunts language use. Daily reference

bleeds into separate and autonomous regions of
likeness, the absence of grass comes to mean

a relation to metallic surfaces that continue to
produce light. Refraction of one or the other

element eliminates the grounds of self, until who
we discern, public in his argument, stands still

at the side of a hillside, working his way through
to the other side, until it too has the opposite

effect and vanishes. We are coming back to
the forum of articulated absence, the ways in which

neither light nor water can produce an effect
that we haven't already inhabited as source text.

The landscape where any of us begins is also
the absence of that landscape. You come back

inside, solitary, the house is a made-up thing
with rooms separated by walls, and the entryways likewise

constructed to perform their duties. What we
do here, how we enter this or that stanza, becomes

incidental, without context. Movement is less and
less able to define the course of a day, as I sit inside

absolute stillness, occasionally catching the flight
of a robin inside the circular span of sun. What adjustment

had to be made, feral, past instruction, to recombine
water and earth, to end at the lake where nightly

I saw confirmation of body's first mystery?
There is no sign but the endlessness of signs. The river

becomes white from an afternoon blaze, then recurs
as simple flux, the way one's hands can produce

paper and ink, kept nearby, local, like a visitant
offering assistance. Low clouds off to the side of

a scene that is replayed for our pleasure. And what
the body does, how it lives inside to redeem

itself: when it lifts its face and leans into a late breeze.
Learning to define what it knows by what it

remembers of the world.

9

Ten months….a year…another decade….
We felt ourselves heavier on earth's surface, bodiless

almost, at each crossing the figurative displacement
of caesura and rest, octagonal light from the west

as I went down to the Hudson's edge, a hawk
wheeling above, distant epochal shifts that assent

to our movement, rescinding segmentation or alignment
to soften one's hands, as if crayon and clay were boated

surfaces of linen. The window that is lighted
mornings I came to sit near the falling curve

of its light that took my eye past Annandale to retreat
where the valley fell among the field flowers of summer.

How does our body return from its occasions, lesser
than what it recalls? I am saved by words that pattern

each page with potential realities, legible spacers in time.
One is listening hard at the door that has just opened, to find

a crossing built from sweet melon and pepper seed, as the palm
opens, divulges its wares, goes stray for a time. Here

in the absolute zero of existence, to halve the numbers
until they vanish again, sixty into thirty into fifteen....

moving to an endpoint as the body is archived, separated
from its history, repeated as ash.

10

Everything passes notice, everything requires a field of
intangibility and sacrifice to become real to itself.

The lateness is less essential than the shape of each
lisp and wisp of dry leaves a daybreak. The skin

shy from contact, retreats, selfish....Separation is
a leaf we've carried in our breast-pocket. One hundred days

are not enough to recover. Earth time saturates the resistant
surface of wood brought inside again. The season

I carve back to find its solitary design. Winter then spring.
Skipping ahead to fall. The slow movement of water

through my hands, as we bend again into the foreign sun. Not
made for this land, I travel back to another, sweetened

from afar by another's age. As if I had become white-
haired and aged in the transition between two fields.

One has no name in this place, no address. The property
is less and less a reason to stay. Dreaming of another

landscape, 'above the peak the moonlight whitens.
A clear wind blows.' As if I were entering a city's port

at daybreak, moving as the wind moves, across the
mountain into the valley to reach open sea again.

11

Evening comes, another in the offing, just past.
Rose of Sharon, growing taller in its second season

still without blooms in late June. Another comes to
tell us of the architecture of light, how it fastens

itself to the ground, spreads across the surface of field
where no one has walked in 30 years. Crossing over

we say it's late to be thinking of free time. Or to
ritualize the elements that provide shelter.

No single bone in my body is holy. I'm less able to
hold your attention, but bring in wine for an evening

of companionship and tired talk, the lake we once
wrote of insists on returning, as the weight of each

monument inside the lit-up scene requires a
new viewing. What resumes are the shadows

we watch with you as the last of the crows depart
into the blue air, recombinant and solitary as they ascend.

Everything has become simpler with time. Going inside
when the need arises, re-emerging at morning. Planting

perennials under the reddening sky. Water and earth
loosened beneath us. Without shame or witness

we pass our days in song. With each day, start over again
rendering the days their due, passing through

to reach Mount Li by nightfall.

23 June-14 December 2020

Convergences

> There is nothing on the tablet of my heart but my love's tall *alif*.
> What can I do? My master taught me no other letter.
>   Háfiz (tr. Elizabeth T. Gray, Jr. and Iraj Anvar)

Yesterday there was this movement after
sunlight across a field that formed

the barest resemblance
to shelter, promising an inclination toward

another's vocabulary, reasserted
here legible an octave below normal

as if to speak were itself reconciliation
with those we'd left behind.

Remembering who I was
when I first wrote these words

'no one is beginning this, language
has become abstraction'

I am learning to translate
objects in natural time: folds of cloth

run through the hands, the presence
of crows enabling the system to

write itself out again, to give thanks
above a crest of northern light

sequestered, pocked, small where
human shelter has vanished.

■

To say the days are coming
through hollowed-out words of survival

written for strangers'
eyes so much remains unseen

To tell this story I need rebab
and harp.

■

Trace the formation of inside and outside, the
work of one's mind moving into and out of

real time. Out to the real, bounded by what relates
one to the other, a lifetime intricately informed

by such movements, startled to recognize the
light in its changes, perceptible as

rain moving from a falling layer of clouds.
Habitation starts in the mind, proceeds

according to one's senses.

■

Across each field, amidst
the statelessness of our person

there is this formation of
interiority as winds travel up from the south

apart from and within what's moving
daylight's advance following a night of rain

here in the aftermath of rain
light leading into color sienna,

turquoise, pitted shale.

▪

To note the clarity of a world at
the water's edge

trout lily, hepatica, bloodroot held
in passing, as if to relate their

presence were to re-create the
pattern by which they came into view.

▪

The way 'you' comes to us inside the
deictic circle, we can repeat its

vigilance even if we can't produce its name.
Birds get fat on autumn grain and beans

dragons are ready to hibernate in cold
waters and sand.

In this world of observances, we're revisiting
landscapes of near-home, combining

our thirst for dew-like flowers

'red in red repetition'
with blossoms along the towpath

gathered under red hickory
and shagbark maple.

■

Reading Du Fu in cold morning light:

'The River draws back, isles and shoals appear,
the heavens are empty, the things of the scene clear.'

As if to readjust sense and sound, to realign
the body with its audition here, a sequence

torn from the banks of an abandoned river.
Their names are part of what we're absorbing, re-

circling, pitch of light when it's dawn
our privacy re-worn, re-won

a category of being that is supple to the touch,
you can inherit its habitation, the spare

room in which we sit, a frame given to us, lexical
time, a border between then and now

that marks each act of observance.

■

But it was this difference, between deictic life
and daily experience that led me back to you

not once but across the days
as I read you from inside a spare room

where light moves in regular intervals
sharper with the afternoon sun

so that the blinds need to be adjusted
keeping the sharpness out, the light

streaming upward to the ceiling.
Daylight's passage to this point, lateness

of each movement, as your hand isn't
yet near nor far, balanced between gnostic rasp

and external shadow.

▪

In any lifetime to recognize the position of
another, to situate one next to the other

as if apposite spirits, craving their same
place on earth's floor. I was situated here

to find you, a student in this discipline
of love, you said you had come to find

hidden here the kernel of truth. Each
separation is a position of unity.

Neither is before the other. Your hand
left on the table a note for me to read

in Cyrillic lettering. My eyes scanned
the heavens for sign of your return.

∎

How many minutes? How many hours
or days? My garden in late summer, moving

into fall, or another season in which I
wander without light of the moon—

to enter the garden at dusk and leave at morning.
Rose of Sharon bush rising, taller by the season.

Field where there was once field passed
over by light storms.

What's available is this version of a world,
no other but this, quieter by the day.

∎

What comes back? Ghazal's intricate form
settles in the mouth, becomes like sweet wine

on the lips, you can move into the space it
creates, let your body rest between *bayts*

cleansed at the end of each day's work.
'Remember the day of union with friends'

It's dark out, the moon yesterday was in
the tree line. 'Although there are always

a hundred rivers in my eye.'
Spotted owls passed through the light.

Let the waters of Zindehrúd come find you.

Waiting and adrift. Was there one answer? Now two?
The light rises in us, to the eyes closes, as it falls

on the deepening surfaces of river.

21 November-15 December 2020

ATTUNEMENT

> Each time a light rises up from you, a light comes down
> toward you, and each time a flame rises from you
> a corresponding flame comes down toward you.
> Henry Corbin, *The Man of Light in Iranian Sufism*

Reading late into the evening a book of translations
from the Persian *I am this*

a woman alone / at the threshold of a
cold season

your eyes and my mouth fused
in this seventh alphabet of late summer

I made myself a partner to your
handwriting, your name written in Farsi

on a bed of winter straw and rice paper.

▪

The lights of connection have gone dark.

I go outside into the wet night, it's warm, the weather
has changed, sunlight where there was grey, now

the orphan hawk spanning his wings
above, in a sea station of blue, I'm reimagining

his return, black object in open space
performing a perfect arc away from us.

▪

The seven moons I can see
from this window

are a kind of separation
of light from object, when the moon

is heavy another comes into view.

Water is spreading itself
across the horizon, the clouds remove the moon

from view when I go out, wait
for the shift to occur

a square of red cloth torn into halves
the halves torn into quadrants.

■

A prayer shawl pulled off the woman's
shoulders and her back

revealed through a wing of
yellow canopy light.

An evening of Sufic prayer.
Her eyes when she turns and sees

it's not one but two who approach,
a duality seen separately

as one then two
form the fold, her eyes that trace

the first from the second, the second
from the first.

Her whole life *as if on an imagined flight path*
each was given its life back again.

∎

What terrified you?

When you saw the body
wrapped in old clothes, what alarmed you?

The emptiness was rhetorical
the body removed for a week

it didn't leave the house but rested
inside until the light came in

the form of a rainbow you saw
pass across the top of the house.

∎

A rainbow body.

And what could be found later?
The body becoming smaller

as the rainbow rose over the house
the body's emptiness rhetorical

reduced to nails and hair.

∎

We gave form to the Etruscan wax as
instructed, guided by mineral stars

in a late autumn sky, watched
as it became like the three-headed

falcon of the sea and on its left
the form of a baboon and on the right

the figure of an ibis.

∎

And we gave it the extended wings that
stretched across its breast

that it could hold its scepter and be
wrapped like Osiris in waxed linen.

The arrangement like folds of
blue skin, bluing at the edges

intact in morning light, we could
disappear into its recitation, an alphabet

inside a heart made of magnetite.

There is light and there is
absence of light.

One makes peace with each
shadow as it comes, as if

days were inexhaustible, one
day following another, the next following.

∎

Reading of the fallen phallus
of Rudra, the cosmic pillar

flaming upward from the netherworld
into heaven

like the counter-player of the light
from beyond. And I could see the pillar

rise in cosmic night in its
splendor from immeasurable depths.

21 November-15 December 2020

II: Collecting the Signs

THE SEPARATION OF EARTHLY OBJECTS

An object is not an object. It is a witness to a relationship.
                                              Cecilia Vicuña

1

An objective understanding....
of rain, the seventh

day without color, a parched space
inside the language pool

light from the stars, a vacancy
at mid-morning, going out and away

from the body

that returns oneself to the sound
of objects, parallel beginnings, tools

we say are here for the keeping....

Begin to offer remonstrance, signs
from Bahia, the signature effort

is to remain
without self among the living, to become

this object among the dying, a wordless
prophecy of oneself passing. A beginning

near the end of one's
abilities. Begin with cloud color

at daylight, no sun but grey stream
rocking the heart

to its very beginnings.

2

The birth of color begins in the entanglement
of water. Color is the birth of light.

Low clouds morning visitation, the words are
forming separable from their origins. Stars

crease the heavens. I have been moving
into their stream, heavenly bodies, the architecture

loose and ungainly. I'm not one but two, the occupancy
of a system, here in the apparel of another's

light, to come down these stairs, dawn
weighted with silver, a perimeter that hooks

sky, bleeds our nights into day. There is this
sanctuary, intricate respite, cut-out, here on the floor

with scissors and paper, the hands are local
to their means, locality is meaning a way of drawing

down the moon, of making its appearance
in a room upstairs, in the way of some going

backward and forward, light that is plurality's
shade, a skinned object holds the jeweled stream

from outside in. To control it one sits here
with the blinds closed, at sundown the house drawn

quiet with blinds closed, in the sunless day the
blinds hold one at a distance from oneself.

3

This is this theory: that some things are not
yet here. The world we are seeing is not yet

here, but the emptiness divides itself, keeps its
daylight to another site. Locust-eyed. A perimeter

cuts both ways, I am starved for this beginning
point, as origin is a taking back, a starting over

inside the dream of another's language. Blue
gentian dusk, fish-eye where color separates…

What comes into the discourse is what separates it
from first denial. Apparitions of water and *quipu*

as if to dream thread were to wear its mark, to waver
above water's line, instrumentalizing the dying

so that they wear their uniforms of abstract liquefaction, bind us to
solstice of the sprit, blanched by this parallel cross, abandoned

where the cross goes blue, the downward crushing of its
synthesis, a work of finite glory. Bowls of gentian and coronal

wafers of light dipped in syncretic ocean light, the realism that is
part and parcel of one's deliverance, as separation moves

across a line seconded by azure, mint and rosemary from the
empty garden that combine as gifts of instruction. One is delivering

tactile messages from beyond an undrawn boundary, to keep the
ground clear of debris, to move among these objects

established in signs beyond oneself: here is a theory of aquatic
travel, blue from the edges, morning of *quipu*

black then yellow dipped in blood.

4

'I was waking outside, the city I had known
when I was younger—

block by block the water had moved thru.'

As if limitation were intricate resolver, a network
of waterways that harbored self and its objects until

referentiality became the problem, the art of saying
out loud to oneself into the dark: 'I haven't a clue where you've gone..'

'I saw you yesterday.' Habit and script aligned, together
the bodily frame becoming a solid wall, blue and

yellow, a wall of blue and yellow one saw from
outside, jonquils and verbena, the shattered cells of ilex

forming a nominal pattern. There is the discourse of memory
and the ritual of object relations. Between them is

the fabrication of god. 'I knelt down and began to
count the stones inside a circle of cut grass.'

Lake and its waters…a shattered ilex….repetition
until one can soften the blow, say the days were already

in progress, no need to recircle them. A sparrow
landing inside the frame, one then another form of

calling, bird and its introit, the grass softer inside these
gardens as I move into the emptiness of tarmac and buildings.

Pressed to acknowledge another's presence, let's say the words retreated
on canvas board, the board bent above a creek that had faltered.

Let's say it's labor all around, that the degree of witness is
several, each instant forming a band, a weathered clip

of color, like arterial lozenges taken into account. The day as
casualty of sight, provenance of sound and in-keeping.

A story, networked, sent into hiding…

5

The religiosity of alienation is its purpose.
Set some things down. Let the role of their emergent

speech retrace then refract reference. Speech
bluer than yellow, green and aqua-marine together, common

daylight, one who appears at the entry way of these
things, aligned with objects left behind, a city in mind, the sidewalks

and avenues they start to become. Each locale emerges
to maintain itself, becoming a public object. One hinges

oneself among these public gardens, black walls inside of green
knots of azalea and goldenrod. The socio-political

germ of river talk. Renegotiating the commons to mend polity.
A scene of enlarged regret, as if inside the place of speaking

a river is moving, the light less and less audible, one
shares some things in common, belief that what sustains

beauty is the same as what objectifies the landscape, marking
each tree line and border in grey. What brings the body back

is syntax, a system of address, fatal in the half light, that one is
with and not with others, retreating and advancing at the same

instant, as if in preparation for the body's departure, so each
is brought here, intricately purposed, to say some things in public

time, the half-hidden, half-announced stages of selecting
what gets said, how light can separate address from tree line.

The singularity of celestial ease is that it is enclosed in language.
Reference is lost mid-sentence, the way we round the circle

of each arrangement, parataxis folded from blue linen,
light that is the separation of body from ground, each view

moving us into the central space again, where we take note
of common objects, sunlight moving across the screen, obliterating

each sign, rows of letters hinged to the temporal yet breaking
back into color, soundless along the river's edge, willow shoots and palm.

There is no lesson other than the one that came to me just now, that
'carmine is a lake of cochineal, derived from the

blood of insects,' as yesterday displacement spoke of the wide
margin of light filtered between window and tree line, the incremental

enactment of polis as silence, a street surrendering to rain, the lateral
motion of water across wood frame, to enunciate one's absence

here, a formative emplacement of otherness
turned toward oneself. Each unit is specified by what

it can't include, the common web of intersecting fields, as if
what brought the day into being were this backyard silence that opens

out, becomes plural, even as daylight pushes the body
out of its hiding space. Water, the irrigated surface, a single

line of thread, pulled into light, cochineal, blood lake,
carmine from the bodies of the dying.

6

Concurrent. Arithmetic for the objective scene.
Weighted by what's common, here in the actuality

of line and argument. There's material below the
surface, a weighted formation, as though one could enter

from the side entrance, sit down awhile, let the fabric
soak up fading color of morning. 'I have circled myself without

finding rest,' each of us in their own time, the pronominal
case that eludes detection, inside and outside combined

to resituate the earthly, reclaim where one sharpens, as evidence
of the found scene goes dark. 'I am certainly more for greatness

in a Shade than in the open day,' voiceless as if to prophecy
one's disappearance. The redness of the light, the casualness

of a field at sundown, one can share its qualities
even as it moves out of view. Less quiet than held

open as visitant, as moral object. The skin loose
at the wrist, the eyes moving toward a tree line that is

articulated by what it doesn't reveal. Each movement
is without form until it becomes an object, moved through

the empathy of thought, weighted by what was said in private, 'river
of me that flows away.' It is the voice dreaming out of itself, sensualist

staring out a window poured from the water's circle, absorbed
as much as lost, so that I find myself moving through each bent

articulation of color, aware that we are encircled
by water, as each margin flooded again, rope that is

both distinct and objectively distant, formed piecemeal in memory
as one can say the hawk moved twice across the same

area of sky. The wind came from the northwest. Edged
by morning light, the bird rose and fell as one bird.

These are parts of what I saw. Coeval with what is
shaded, crayoned out: the bird body as scriptural, silenced

by what it can't remove or destroy.

7

To grow old with them—aromatic thyme, marjoram and violet beds—
to see the years shaped by what they provided. Not here but where

I was going to be. A situation not a place. The objects of
a lifetime inserted, re-invented, re-traced beginnings

from inside the colored light, beaded, intricate, like a
Granada sunset, the pluralism of oneself as if any day

were vehicle and sounding board, not tree or rock
but a wave, movement of systole and diastole, rising

and falling. Balletic, my body moves into its position
of speaking from inside a pattern. The red lines into which

I cast my common voice. Inherited to say
what is coming, what happened, what the next object

will become before it disappears. As fable, formed on my lips
apart from any audience. So, the risk is of silence

out of sound, an alphabet from inside the web of relation
that is neither self-same nor outer. On a backdrop

of enormous emptiness to scratch out these few
designs, let the fabulist ring move into its radical

outer circle, wave and cycle, cycle and wave, the
designation of saying that marks temporality, achieves

haven out of earth knots, wood from the wood
pile, brought inside, laid on wool carpets, the reticence

and industry of song, built inside one's habitat.

8

A plane of experience awakened by what can't be recalled.
'I was going nowhere, I sat down on the edge of a

riverbank, I was going nowhere, I sat down....'
So that the rites of separation are indigenous, field

and sign of field made one. A compact, companion
leaves, these indices of having been.

No place is without precarity. At the hinge point
between disappearance and fate, the objective is to

redress absence. The history of a self that is the humming
of one then two birds, the common actuarial beginning

of movement, one then two, the relation of separation
to *ecstasis*. Not morning or evening but their calligraphic repetition.

Mottled board, glue, loose cotton bunting. Signs
apart from their objects. The readability of facial gestures.

Cool throat, wetted tongue. Bird talk at the margins.
I'm laying these objects in line, the implicative gesture

that is several times over the same one. 'You write
for no one' or the daylight is estranged from what it reveals.

'Each sentence is the beginning of the same gesture.'
Word rites, combining what comes from outside into a

field I went to nearby, low-lying clouds that emptied
out over each deserted building. Not the sun but the wind

giving sign of its presence. A saturation point, daylight when I
return to the work room, balletic field song, I sat down

inside a yellow curtain of light, crepe myrtle outside, reddening
until I couldn't see it anymore, curtain of half-light, realism's

blue shade, mortal, impervious to any living object.

9

In paratactic resolve, the emptying and the
emptying again of the singular. Gestures from a

field that falls away, the separation of bodies
moving singular, separately, aligned across a line

of vision. The emblemizing of their enabled situated
selves, one walking separate from the other, relational

histories of subjective life, their retracing as signatory, aslant, grief-
stricken or mourning-less. As common beings, their

persons entwined, they can say 'this happened' or
'this won't happen again.' A casuistry of tactical knowledge

like rinsed boards left outside in a windstorm, the yellow marks
of water along the grain, one hand then another carries

the boards out to another part of the field. This is solitary
work, the otherness of a partition that enacts

in seriatim these planes of experience. 'Here in the oblong
lot I was watering a line of flowers.' Adhering to the objective

cadence, its inhered dissipation, dissolving like bark bits
in a bucket of water, the order of stairs and stars, a repetition

that initializes activity, as my eyes turn from one window
to the line between my two hands. Sentence by sentence

listening for their voices inside my own leaving and coming
to one's senses in a paradigm of outlooking, these noticings

moved from one locality to the next, companionable and
inseparable, as the subject is an object divided by what it is divested of.

The carved brass left at the bottom of the river, Oshun's
tale I'm reading against the light, the objects she took

to the bottom of the river, sign's appearance in river
air, blue where the sediment is rising up to our waists, cool

Iworo bird with brilliant plume on her head, the appearance
of objects that are twinned, Iworo bird and plume, the gathering

together of an image, as water is cooler at the bottom, when the river
lowers itself and the body is lowered into it, water when the waist

is burdened by its motility, soundless, as one is carrying
brass into the circle, wave and cycle of water, the yellow

grass when Oshun is moving, out of sight, inside the
circle, a span of one's good eye, two good eyes, the bird and its cloth

marker, threaded blue *quipu* from earth's shoulder, as shade
and bird are two things, the water from her mouth

both salve and sealant, both cure and cause, marine line
of red wings, bird that is rising, involuntarily, one morning after another

a ringed aftermath of light
a jeweled body that moves toward you.

13 September 2022-3 January 2023

Autobiography of Spirit: Novitiate Series

1

Daily life you said has become the norm, as if
to lie down were the same as to sit up, take in

the room where existence happens again.
We are lighter, leaning into a slight wind, the way earth

light transports us, built out of units of experience
we call sight. Vision commingles, re-creates

surface life, situated here, inside the appearance
of another era. Time advances, no way to kill

it but situate the body, loose clothing, workman's
outfit, go into it, release the skin to light

as the plurality of subjects encompasses us
against all possibility of return. Here is one

slant of light, we are private selves here again
but the light is public, it disowns our individualism

at every turn. If we turn away....the route
less clear, so that we can't hold ourselves here

in this space anymore, the world becoming
intangible, removed from our public selves.

Tree line in late sun is a sign of change, as if
what came before was another tree line

and this one had become renewed in perception
that is without memory's laws yet instantaneous

with what preceded it. We can't assume the days will
continue, the harmony and symmetry of this world

may dissolve tomorrow, yet the light from inside a curtain
curves around oneself, like a beam from outside

that stills us, keeps our body from moving out. Under
is inner, the spirit is trellis and vine, collapsed into

the idiom of a survivalist. What did Virgil ask us
to see: *taeda* in a black grove, the emptiness

of each line, to re-articulate form at the base of these
hills, regarding the passage from one to the next

the way observance yields evening fires that pour forth light.

2

Avalanche country, like bear country.
The threat hardly ever comes but

it defines our place on this ground. Fear
that comes from inside the space we're

watching for a change in light, afternoon
summer, the endings of a storm that's passed.

What do I do here? Come back, raised
arms on a chair inside, the outside is there again

where my body was 10 minutes ago. Here
is another....Each is here, a kind of graphemic

representation of this place, now another, seamless
as histories are mobilized to have us return

across one field, where water was, then no
water we can see. What did Thoreau notice

in his journal, 'the ripples sparkling in the sun'
that reminded him of a correspondence to

ice waves, the 'erect ice flakes' he understood
as completing a vision that brought two

planes of sight into one corresponding image.
My hands from inside my jacket 37 years ago

rummaging now, to collect rocks from my
garden after a rainstorm. The erect slant

of sunlight that moves west to east in this sudden
emptying out of light, pure gravel on the floor

of a garden bed, the light moving across it.

3

The separation is a terminus, a bridge and aftermath
of bridging. I took my walk out to the field

behind our house, quiet skies, no one seeing me
come or go. Was it once like this or did another

say, 'You're right, the road to the east, you can go
from there to this other one and come back here.'

Somehow to be in the middle of it is to name
the site where it wasn't a thing but a collection of things

separated from vision. Tagged tree line, the skin
slighted by a rainstorm, now comes to rest

inside a line of sight. Body is a thing moving, we're less
careful to note what it does, water on the tongue

all day long the collapsing of the symbolic
world into these objects of notable emptiness.

It's not in vain the mind turns this way and that
in search of analogy, a river that is moving as I might

have seen it move, once in writing about it, in Ohio
at the edge of that moon shot light, ahistorical

yet framed by what materials provided me. The
taste of salt, wet cotton, inside a nest of phenomenological

containment. My name experiences a lag between
what it can do and what it will say. Here in the

séance I'm listening for our dead, inside Ohio's
water, the bridge I am seeing forming in my mind

without preference or prediction. Everything is saturated
in the dusk when it appears again, bridge and light

from the bridge. A circle of invented exactness.

4

So it can be mediated, translated into new song
as memory elicits content that is ready to go outside….

What Olson recalls, records in *Maximus*, that he
saw 'the moon / now gone a quarter toward / last

quarter comes / out' as if moon and object
were the same, the mantic distress of symbolic

night worked out as objective reality. The dark
light, one says it's already here, inside the left side

of your chest as you feel the weight of it, all day
through the evening, into this one residual

undoing. Land is here, there, the window open
to a day that comes back inside. Weather

looser than we remember, able to re-translate
horizon so it goes blue when the shade tree in

the yard shakes in a hard pre-storm wind. Rose
of Sharon in the front pulled down to the ground

rises, raised by another wind from the west.

5

If movement were this simple…here against the wall
of the cemetery, at the back, where low lying trees

merge to form a horizon across the landscape.
The shifts are variable, calmer then loose bits of

light tagging roofs. A shield inside the daylight
that draws off water. I'm writing from inside

to you on the outside. My yearly occupation
here again a kind of circle, the marking down

of time, working out its channels, as my
mother sat in Brighton one morning and forced

her own mother to retreat underneath a wave
of light. 'She was startled to see me,' said Iris.

The days don't care. We can be or not be.
Someone once came past, proposed limits to what

any of us could forecast. 'My pen is a lever'
Thoreau writes, 'in proportion as the near

end stirs me further within.' What
escapes notice....The sparrows are back

at the feeder, light spreads unevenly across
the white back of a neighbor's house.

Foreground and background merge, simple
methodology of light. To retrace its

canonical effects, its diurnal frame. Each
flower and leaf lit from the outside.

27 October 2020

Field Notes from a Light Storm

> The flowers burst out of the ground overnight. Those flowers have cool light colors. Only the stars resemble them. You leave the house one morning, you go out onto the plains, straight ahead for there's nothing anywhere, nothing but the horizon and the same horizon beyond the horizon. You're alone, alone like....Ah! I can't really say like whom, like what.
> Victor Serge, *Midnight in the Century*

What draws one
out, nightly the position

the body is taking
upon itself to

recur in place
as if brought

without care
to this

site...earth worn
grafted

artifact of another's
struggle to cohere.

■

'Alone also with the horizon. The waves
come from the invisible East, patiently,

one by one. A long voyage, with no
beginning and no end...Rivers and

streams pass by, the sea passes and
remains. This is how one ought to

love, faithful and fleeting. I wed
the sea.'

∎

I wed the sea that held me...

the justice of its
tides movement that is

both allusive and real
so that one is taken

out of himself
replaced by wind & spray

dark ribbons of salt.

∎

It is pure conjecture
force of will

to inhabit this body
recognize

simplicity in no
movement at all

ungainly with age
my father rose

in dawn light

threaded through windows
of our shared

two-story home

'I am going to leave the paper
for you to finish.'

His words
like a coterie

of thought
cut from fresh

light.

∎

'Thought is outside
itself, but remains

marvelously in
itself, or returns

to itself.'

To starve
in the house of thought

What does
the body

recognize as
its own?

My hand
lifts a cup to drink

without thought.

A companion
drifts

sits nearby
remembering what it was

points us
there

tones of the greater world.

▪

The partnering

of light morning
saffron light the skin

deluged in warm
sun. The mouth of

my beloved a crescent
moon lingering

in the western sky.

▪

Yet what you
remember

is not shelter—

low-lying coast you can't name
or regard the water's shine

at 6 o'clock
in June

your head capped
by an orange

discus of light.

∎

What was it gave one back
their age the even stare

of eternity?

∎

We said it was
this world we didn't

know another to you
we are this one thing

built on top of other
things reading the world

for signs as Virgil
proposed—

'By fixed and sure signs
we are able to learn all this:

spells of heat and rainfalls and winds
driving in the cold.'

∎

Reading the world
as signs

from theft's cup
of wonder

'cranes into the air have
fled from the

rising rain
out of canyon floors'

Temporality's star-
crossed lover

scuttling each
formation.

One lives
inside these momentary

lapses
kindred spirits

hovering just
above the horizon.

∎

The ocean sinks
into the fabric, skin

& salt, sea &
light....

shells and beads
collected among strangers.

30 December 2019

Four Georgics

1

As dream so the common
day is borne, sweet bay, poet's

laurel, to encumber *Laurus nobilis*
as *alloro poetico*, resemble what's

crossed-out, cut over, instructs the now
time, not yet time, of winter, to

gather acorns and laurel berries
like the cherries one is darker

than red, the color of one's
hands in winter, the color

of the cherries and young
elms, to winter where the red

day is dawning, in shadow, to
fit one's mother's tongue, a

dormant Parannasan bay
that also grows in our

mother's shadow.

*

Shape is conventional.
Say the turn is relinquished

as speech, to reconstitute
rosemary, bay or myrtle, in

white days to resurrect these
unrelated, grown them at the

end of a summer noon, say
one is in shadow, the sucker

from the base of the old
tree weathered, whitening

as *laurea folia*, as red deepens
branched leaves of bay medicinal

for cattle.

2

Not single in kind, as nettle or
branch, *celtis australis*

the sturdy elms or the willow
and lotus, to sing serial

distinct from *paliouros*, a bird
wrenched from sky, distant

as clay, umbral light reaches surely
underneath, as the lotus

tree beares a fruit bigger
than pepper, refines

sweetnesss, red sky to late
day root, one is at the margins

of each, in the shape of the
leaves, their margins and veination

between species, recur as wood's
acumen, musical phases

translated out of turn, the blest
resemblance of leaves, to fold

common leaf with nettle, black sky
as storms remain hidden from

view, a day later the wood
transparent, musical in its

instrumentation.

3

Low smoke, shelled elm, written to
recur, common ground or field

as one names it, *ulmus capinfolia*
that accepts the form of the

crooked plow, breaks incipient
earth, squall birds rose colored

as with others like the cherry
and elm, a very dense thicket

recurs, nominal sloped hand
that takes the breaking plants, in a

dense undergrowth, to reach
inside the single leaf, as if

denissima silva were cherry shot
up from the root, skilled

plant lifts itself out, rain
cover when July, so rich

in leaves, combines cover
with joyous vines, elements

of change, planted in line
wood used for bent work

of shipbuilding, where Cato
indicates *bubus pabulum*

cattle fodder, the distinct
training of elm saplings, new

comme-out leaves & used for
sawce like pothearbs.

4

As recurs in nature, field of
ilex, scented holly oak, holm

oak, *quercus ilex*, as rites speak
of shell & heart, built from slow

mended winter, the work to remain is
lower than here, Silarus crest

of green, the séance left un-
tended in spring, one says the

day is shorter, where Alburnus is
green with holly oak, to build

as bees hide their swarms in the
hollow shell and heart of a

decayed holly oak, some common
adaptation, builds under, water

as oak trough, residual ilex
amid flavor of rain, sweet to drink

the water running through
oak, *aut sicubi nigrum*, make

where one is a dark grove of
dense holm oak overlays, wind

rest not so great as wet leaves
scorched by sun, duration of rain

and oak weed across corn, as rain scores
branches of slashed oak, surface

and interior darkened by leccio
that flows back inside, current of water

run its course, the rain as
acorn wash, berry-like red

gall of solarity.

23 May 2022

EARTH LIGHT, EARTH SOUND

> Creation myth is a paradox. It is a vision of catastrophe and of coherence-in-depth nevertheless within or beneath the fragmented surfaces of given world orders.
> Wilson Harris

1

Walking is a way of world-making, as though
thought were indelible. Snow crest on the

border, the wings of an angel, one can say
the truth is made underneath, diversionary

by turns, so that the signs of regret are leveled
on a city street, black where the trees end

in a row. This romance of the ritualized, imperfect
recollection, like the rough stones gathered

from the sea, one can total them, six times
seven, the arrangement coming up the same

time after time. This mastic mathematics
performed in the dark, one is left to believe

in such small things, to encounter the drum
next to a desk, winged aftermath of the retrieved

language that draws itself inward.

2

And the day is signpost to what ends it, what realizes
time in the hidden instant of collection. Mind is

blank where the hands go under, dark as a space
inhabited by atomic particles loosened against

one's body. The birth of that instant, mound after
mound of earth, the elastic simplicity of the formation

that follows, enabling 'what swiftness of movement
has been granted to the particles of matter….'

Like delirium before one passes into its objective
silence, the inheritance of their movements, to realize

that each hour is this shared space of time, this conjoint
witness, hovering near the surface, like a betrothed

sister, this kindred spirit, inside the cut, 'when dawn
sprinkles the earth with fresh light and the variegated birds

flit through the delicate air, filling the pathless woods
with liquid notes.' It comes back, inside the tinfoil

register, that the hand is human, the wing is cut
from wire, the enabling instinct of which is to freeze

each movement above the other, to locate where one
is by what the mouth has devised, silence, beginning

inside moon's plastic light, mooring at a distance, serrated
where the wind is taking your voice, moon-lit

like a sphere raised to the heavens.

3

Where we can join Lucretius, simply join where
he is, the anything of saying that becomes a

practice, wielded in silence with oneself, the object
of beginning to order the pieces, the rising sun

at times filling the woods with noise, plastic light cells
that crease and delineate the border, one's body

lifts, is brought back, toward the ending of another's light,
the particles of heat rising, then abeyant, subsumed

by interiority, as if the wings were amassed in stone, the planted
rock form of their solid and simple travel, to await them

at the rock's end, rook's rain, sweet water melted on
grey-faced rock mass, to end there, against one's will

like a body in motion, sunlit, racing through time.

4

There is this surplus, the rain is based on water
when it falls, the water on light, floating between

the surface and an adjacent river. Nothing can become
what it is until it has transformed itself, material

existence in the exigencies of light. The interlacement
of shapes that become vehicles of sound, tropic

instruments of light and movement, as if one could
travel inside each stream, separated from what once

gave it unity. When one knows that the universe has
no bottom, no place where the ultimate particles

can settle, so that each pond is creased by what enters
it, pool of matter that is suspended just above

the falling surface, each locale pierced by what enunciates
its ending, flesh intricately bound to what is

not flesh, the order of which is to settle again, to retrieve
sound from the solitary movement of particles, their

intricate register of falling and rising, like 'unsubstantial
falling and rising light.' A room with its windows thrown

open onto a field, the field thrown open onto its opposite, hill and
river bound by the single stream of sunlight, apparent

as any composed bodies inside a wheel of light, blue black
and falling where the light falls.

5

To cut the body from its insides visit
the station where it appears....

What appears as inside, what travels
from one end of the body to the

other, ministered, clotted, blood
in the lung, like a low cloud

floating over the Euphrates.
What hinders passage, becomes

blue estrangement, elements of
passage like a harmed idiolect

captured from the river bottom.
To retrieve memory inside the hill

where the body was brought. Hill
side where the body was shaved

then left to dry, the insides poured over
the out, to hear them collect

it again, the men beating their
breasts, their clothing loosened

in this early stage of mourning.

6

There is this remainder like water
that passes through a hook, toward another's

body, the hook that is passed through light
across a steering wall, the weight of each

hand over the corpse, this longitude spread
out across the sloping curvature of torso

painted on wet wood. The name is carved
from another's name, the wood wetted

by paint, spread out over the body, to enlighten
the dead with paint, to redress death by offering

another in its place. They extract the brain
by passing a hooked iron instrument

through the nostrils; part of the brain
is extracted, meditation of the first border

cut from its flesh, when they open the side
of flesh, cut into it with a sharp Ethiopian

knife, parallel to the root, the body cut
from its stance as material, then cleaned

with palm wine and spices. This rhythmic
birth root that is spread out on the floor

of earth and leaves, so that one moves
within the shadows of the equinox, an embattled

spirit, caught between worlds, its body wrapped
in bandages, strips of balsa and linen, cut

into straps, bound into the earth gouge, written
out of existence by what materializes it, black

clay, straw, a gourd of light.

21 March 2018

III: SENTENCES FROM A SENSUAL EARTH

MOURNING: A WORK SONG

> And grass, and white and morning glories, and white and red clover,
> and the song of the phoebe-bird...
> Walt Whitman

1

To journey toward oneself
away from others. What is matter?

What is habitat? A wheel of light
in the yard, the opening of an eye

as litmus test of the real. Not spool
but splay, attending to separation

as common root, figure of one
in the nests of sparrows and finch.

One lacks sincerity, the other
moves out of sight. Wayward pitch.

A glimpse of untimely death.
To pry the bird from its nest, box

of feathers, skin and bones, one
kneels proximate to each body

as though clothed in sunlight.

2

Nocturnal drift....as if passenger
on a boat heading east. The water

below is heaven, the water above
another form of light. Seriality

sheds companionship for the days
ahead. I'm listening to the bird

cries outside, the infinite
possibility of sound to replicate

this inner earth, this enacted
site of reparation. 'The air

full of invisible bolts,' as the
book enters a dream I am having

in conversation with a woman who has
been dead for 37 years...another

visitor waits beside her to carry the
body back from its burial site.

Every path belongs to these waters
enfolding two, then three, one

then none. The encounters divergent
and recursive, not revealing themselves

as logos but imprinted, brighter
where the light has moved off-center.

So that one can hear
the red-winged robin cross over

each fold, April's light forgiving
ambient, indirect.

3

Endless unfolding of works.

I have sat down amid the rain
storms to read Hölderlin.

'The stalks of life breathe more fiery
in the shadows of the vine. But

it is a beautiful thing to unfold
the soul and this brief life.'

The idiom is familiar, mottled red
skies, I turn down the shade, let the

outside unsettle my body, the clarity
of language creating a movement

that I can find kinship in. 'No
stranger form than the one you make.'

As sky turns red then black, in the
southwest the clouds are moving

across, tree by tree, each sign
falls into the open air, my lungs

expand, whipped by wind, as
red turns to black, sky folds

about its hill, wind and color
wrapped around a birdwing.

4

So many dead roped together, like
rocks placed in a field of red flowers.

Eternity isn't here, or there
but inside our earthly habitat, shaped

from a wing brought close to one's
eye. Here is closure all over again, witness

and thirst, a body that receives its
human host, shatters on contact with

river and dark green lightning. The field
is and isn't allegorical, the night I

keep inside my shirt, a shelter of
ribbed plastic, skirt lit by human elders

shadowed inside sundial foam, rhetoric
of thrust and parry, for how many

years in a row, the scale of surface
received, handled, re-drawn like the

liquefaction of canyon and desert flower.

5

'I' am coming close to 'I' as any next I
meet is waiting, driven, sorted by its

nominative power to unbend, breathe
near flower and sweet mead, the essential

carpentry as flower and sign
are released into the world.

Recursive yet restive as days are longer to summon
urgency. The dreamt of particularity of spring

that is looser, a model of restraint. Not shy
but stammering part way through the door's opening.

A sky less and less able to govern conduct below.
But Heaven made both, we are reminded, impossible

to begin without direction. The wet rain, black clouds
from a spring storm, even the scattered

thunder, renews the understanding that here
is simply extinction's date, drawn above

a door of homelessness.

6

Gratitude that any one is still present.
Cathexis of each movement. Turn away, the other

is turning toward you. Lift oneself against
light, its granular vocation, as if to separate

objects from perception. One by one
the loosened form of humility, an address

turned away mid-sentence. How many
days you wandered past Potomac's edge

waiting for that tonal affect, as light
is enmeshed in each branch of the real.

Not slope but canyon at the edge of sight.
There you said is the point, as if to supplement

one's ability to fly....

I came to rest inside a shelter like this one,
barely able to talk. Phrases pulled from a book

of plant and tree names, how did I cordon off
what came to represent the self or its journey

across a map of trisected color. My locale a bird's
eye view of ahistorical preamble. To talk

where the days end, each established as
locus and spacer between here & there.

So that we can't know ourselves until we
speak, a chasm between this silence & that

next to a river, red sky, the litmus of belief
attuned to astonishment. Nor do we

speak without housing ourselves, patient
among tall grasses outside York, Pennsylvania

so that to inventory what it means, foliage
and cracked ceiling, the cement walk

I came down, then ran away from, each a
temporal separation, a work resumed by its

economy. As dusk is a transitional sun
that shares our works, voluble skin that situates

the body outside its habitation, Sarasota
light from inside the carryover bluing

of heron & palm, 'the immaculate, the merciful good'
collected in one's hands like cherry blossoms

remote to the touch, sweet frame of a door through
which the dead came to speak.

7

As sweet clover is re-imagined, built
into the day, myrtle blossom that survives memory

to reside here, inside this milky stall, shrub
trefoil, common clover, and salt grass.

The hand can't arrive before it's replaced
by memory of movement, shale rock beneath

one's right foot, the wind of *cystum lotosque*
regional in its emphasis. Each can be

imagined, re-inserted by hand, the way
soil carries inside it seed and shell, blue

veined loam, the rhetorics of its fashioning
empeopled by what is buried there.

As memory is a crossing over and into the built
lair of September, when the pond overflowed

and the coin floated, like a chip of ice, inside
the circle, shadow and coin brought together

by one principle: to see is to salvage seeing.
Each movement crosses over, the hand brings

itself to the face, mnemonic gesture that is
neither pond water nor coin, separated

from the surface, as skin is collaged
from all that penetrated its surface

a body reflected as light and shadow.

8

As the sequence forecasts its ending
among the river plants. Oneself is never here

or elsewhere, to be forgotten, re-made, citizen
as container, the objects of a lifetime inserted

into its frame. This is polity's miracle, stray bits
of life, refined here, gathered by others. The namelessness

of one, empathy produces anonymity, colored
light, the wind across one's hand at sunrise.

Going toward these things, as if clothed in their
habitat were protection and meaning at once, the holy

unseen, imperfect, as skin loosens, the frame dismantles
itself, not light but spectacle, the body leveraged

for its salt, a corpus in hiding. What returns
to our view: the vineyard Hölderlin saw, a bank of

vines across the landscape, which looks
coal-black around this time of autumn.

Understood as labor, the surface is less real
than accepted, stalks of weeds that underwrite

the process, named for what isn't practiced. A year
opening into this meadow, this re-assembled

surface of vine and cloud cover.

9

And the indefinite 'I', ekphrastic, regionless
register of multiple beginnings….

All of it incidental to trauma. The work of one
to re-name themselves. Here the skin is less

motile, reacts less quickly. Turns toward the
low ridge of light, separate from building or

sky, the red register of multiple beginnings…
Charged with one day, how many yet to come.

Recall that one sat here once, as another
came to pass, recall the depths one made of

each subject, turning toward their partner how many
idiolects passed between them. The common

habitat sluiced by motion, subjugated by
daily reports. A low ridge of yellow flowers

one is returning to report they haven't yet
turned, are part too of a system of

recovery, as any injury shifts toward another
for voice. Realism turns away to face itself, not say

what it meant but what it could no
longer hide from view.

10

Impossible to say, the view is gone, sun
falls across men's and women's bodies

where no one is standing. The year is less
than an hour, something said next to one's partner

vanishes, slow to fathom its meaning....
Light empties from the sky, the ending of

day is this common piece. The world
diminished as separation becomes the residual

toil of experience. I gathered my things, someone
remained inside the house, another stood

at the edge of a garden. The periphrastic
situatedness of each body. We can find no

other alternative but to stare back, forward
of belonging, not so much agentless but smaller

as I say these things. As geese gather in the late
sky and the system of their flight is bound

to a network of sound and color, black on
blue, the ribbed internal structure

of flight that connects wing to air. So much
is given, the reddening sky is common to see

yet estranged, partly visible here on
earth as lore, the fiction of historied

living among encampments, temporary
shelter, vacated quarters of inside & outside

slanted to receive the morning rain.

11

Later the partition is less visible.

Vision is crossed, scrolled over, as screen
time settles into a rhythmic field of action.

Mnemonic re-ordering of what was just
said, not settled but fine like loosened

soil across one's hands. Residual
effects, nothing is less than what carries

water inside it. Wind music. Storage
site. The planted visibility of wind chimes

from a distance. Rose on the vine, another's
hand appearing as lattice, raised surface

on white paper. Seasonal skin, the hand
retraces what it can't say, every effort to re-do

the real, as though the body were lifted
from nature, licensed by language to retrace its steps.

Nothing can confirm sea light inside
one's hands, the ribboned salt flecks

that gather there, composite streams of
red curbstone and hydrangea leaves.

Octagonal light that appears inside a
circle of blue horizon, carried forward

isomorphs of travel.

29 May-2 June 2022—28 December 2023

Late River Song

> such a distance I
> have come   to admire
>   the asters here where
> once we lived   but already
> the blossoms have passed their glory
>   Kokinshū

1

One road is working its way up through
consciousness as though bird song were the

exemplar of June when June is still a month
away. To talk here, destabilized, not near

morning but part of the system that organizes
daylight. Color is a song at rest when the

birds are long gone. We are less sure that they
will return, even as sparrow and cardinal arrive

without ceremony. The hawk flies over us
sky and pitch are no nearer for having

located us here.

2

Every song reaches its nadir to arrive
again where it began. You can recognize birth tones

in the smooth anthracite, black rock that is level
with root formation. One remembers

little of how they got here, through this or
that telling, the impermanence of any narrative

each can remember. What was heard
came from another time, route less steady

than proscribed, as each received what they could of earth's
minerals and fruits, as complex daylight striated

palms in late shadow. Everything is less recognizable than
the language that came before it. 'Five zones

comprise the firmament, of which one ever
blushes under the flaring sun, ever scorched

by its fire.' The density is compact, light and its
zonal creation lending space to begin again.

3

'The green mountains are pale
and without charm,' while I live far

from mountains and haven't traveled outside
the area in months. I recognize the crepe myrtle

still out of season, that a layer of frost would invade
the senses all over again, late spring would

refuse the possibility of a second view. Here inside
the room is imperishable light, while outside in the

late afternoon sun a lone pigeon on the lawn
wanders out of view, supplying a cadence that is

not unlike the liberation that comes from palms
laid on a table at dusk. I can't measure the contact

anymore than I can retrace the fingers' depth from
one circle to another. 'The visit is forgotten

and life goes on.' Or the angle resists classification as
one's body is re-measured, re-appropriated, put to

work against its will.

4

'The fragrance recognizable
repeatable as blossoms from
an ancient fig'

To recognize these patterns
of organic material....
Each bend of light particular

A labor that takes place
at the edges of sunlight
moving across our room...

The poem takes up space
in the world, light is taken
from each object in a room

overwhelmed by color.

I get up, I go out, I come
back in... Recognition is a pattern
steadily making its way into

a world of color and objects.
'Magnolia no side
of a boat,'

we leave ourselves
adrift with its signs
of passing, in rows coming

back to drink wine
from a cup left out
overnight. You are

saying there is language inside
the book and there is
language outside of it.

5

Our boat of shato-wood and its
gunwales are cut magnolia.

We hear them passing, one by
one the earthly messengers

are enlisted, something like care
emerges, as robin song is

perpetual inside the boat, though
it's the captivity of movement

we can't let go of. The way
rain that isn't yet part

of our grammar has already
settled on the yard.

One can say they are
'rich for a thousand cups.'

Boards placed inside a carefully
lit room and the light is balanced

all over again. We carry the boards
back inside where another sits, her

arms placed on a table that is
reddish brown wood, and outside

it is another light burning from the
east, bold and yellow as a gull's wing.

The woman wanders away, returns
places the bowl in the center

of a red circle, another lifts her
weight from the bed, becomes weighted

as if moon light were a source of
deliverance, the night a turning spire

in spring grass.

6

The world is made up
of these same pieces, the fabric

looser around one's frame.
Go into it, the days are empty

for oneself. Another is kind
and lies down next to the first.

A body is so many actions
in place. The skin can recall

little of what enacted its
reception. Color moves

across one's hands, darker
among the veins, rich peat

of the knuckles. Each
moves apart from the other.

Each is an object situated
just north of one's wrist, west

of another's torso.

7

There is no journey
you haven't renewed, loose
among the branches…

whitened, you too are
part of the eco-system
a garden, summertime, grey

sparrows resting on an iron
plant hanger, one is lessened
by the weight they bear

in a world of movement
outside. The answer I hear

is terraced, blade by blade
the winter grass goes
straw-like into a cool wind.

'The Sun's gone South,'
bearing a sign of unlimited
expectation. 'How many

thousands are prepared
to dance Him
North?'

8

Light that enters from the east, river
passes beneath a bridge, southwesterly

winds arrive. Fern and lilac in profusion
along the shoreline. I am walking west

with the water, light creases
across the horizon, lowlying

clouds, as limbs of trees
lean across. Tree line

and horizon. Askew
as vision tilts. Robbed

of light, the hands are
dispartnered here. A layer

reddens across the line.
One moves into the water

without effort, hands
reaching for a shelf of elm.

Bluebird in the tree. A
crow cawing from the other

shore.

9

The littlest objects
find new use. Pencil case
stripped wire, shoe cream tin.

The eastern wind without
shadow or rain. Calm
day to move about.

Remembering the story
of Cato in Dante, brought
forward as a suicide

notable for that fact.
I am carrying this image
into the days, weather-beaten

eye that opens to these
mysteries. Cloth draped
onto a chair, safekeeping

I am leaning into the lessons
of a lifetime, lifting them
one by one, the story is

recognizable, fabulous, part
real, part spectral, that to come
here is to see Cato's image

scattered across wet grass.
A tongue cut from its
owner, the blood may still

support life.

10

I am carrying rope, you are saving
       scraps of cloth & twine.
    The work is endless, you wrote, long
days pasting the materials down.
       Collage-work, you said, is

mutable music, the sharing of
       edges, tonal, so that they
    drift end to end, the colors absorbing
sound along the way. Pattern is ongoing
       patience turned

toward itself, as though river water had
       flowed beyond its borders, taken shape inside
    one's extended hands, to rest there
untellable as grass. The calling was this fortune
       throw the dice again and again

    without standing clear on a clear morning
          like this one, the ground cover
        lifted from wads of yellowed stamps, masking
tape, spirals of ribbon laid end to end on
        a green floor.

    *

As each movement
became a form of realism

Eros
binding the words together

colors on the page
the loose shape of a hand

or bird wing, filtered, re-invented
torqued for travel.

And the days could proceed
welcomed for what they connoted

of death, the other side
of our imagination.

As stars may rise
above the river, one's good eye

settle for a point
near recognition's palm.

Sere and slope of line
that is itself a cut inside the field.

Rain makes a place for shelter
to come back into view

Ailanthus and periwinkle.
Geranium and parsley.

A continent inside a field.
Dark green as my hands count

days back to zero.

6 May-14 December 2020-17 June 2022

Nocturnal Suite

> Above, there is the vision of all the heavens contain: sun, moon, stars, constellations of the Zodiac, houses of the moon. Now, you see and discern nothing whatsoever or something that it is like: the precious stone sees only the mine from which it originated, it yearns and is homesick for that alone.
>
> Najm Kobrā

1

The common fire is night, a shadow that
is part of one's make-up, scenic

sidereal shadows that line the mind, as if
to limit sight were the provenance

of one's forgiveness. 'What you said when the trees
lifted into view, like poles stripped of their

becoming, two became four, then infinity....'
this coupling, light & gesture that is both

bodily and work of the waking self. To re-enter
the pulse of each day, when it

is impossible to journey back, see its surface,
supernal, laid across a bridge in

Ohio springtime 40 years ago. As though
incantation were re-creative, a pattern that

proposes this ludic ring, revenant station of
crossing again..... 'streams and spring

that call to allay thirst....' The lying down
at the end of a field, part of the prehensile

pattern of beginning over, landing inside
what is before us, 'the wet rocks all

green with moss and dripping with moisture'
in a recital of one made two.

A body carried back inside its tent, lifted
from what came before it as if for the first time: this

abode of light and dark, systemic, cool to the
touch, blinded by what it cannot yet relate.

2

A finch at evening, the blue-eyed robin
landing at the edge of the garden....I want

to combine these beginnings, eradicate division
between sense and being, the attention

we give, momentary, to hold to a pattern
reintroduced: a sentence lifted from another

text that proposes the way forward into this
realm. 'Night covers the earth with its vast

pall, either because the sun, on reaching the
farthest verge of the sky at the end of his

long course, in exhaustion breathes out his
fires, which have been impaired

and weakened by the journey through so
much air...' The emptiness of one's

being that is flush with the distance between
return and revival, a creative longitudinal

dark that is both ancient & newly born, span
of a lifetime that is bridge to what

foretells it, season after season, the will to
resume what was cast off, sent back, hidden

inside a night rain, local, overcast where sky
turned grey, a shift in color that marked

the site of letting go.

3

What blacks out is what remains
unseen. Sentenced to what wasn't

initially noticed: October sky, beneath
Hunter's Moon, the stars of Cetus and Pisces

condensations of celestial fire, slow-forming
movement of the hands that grasp their

alternative station: placed near water, cool
to the touch, rock separated from ground

lifted by what comes from inside, a slow
forming wave of movement, guided back

by an angel's tongue. What can be heard
again is what plays back of each song, this revival

of skin's habitude. What did Hölderlin
call it, 'this floor of being…native woods

and smoke….by the fig tree' we saw
from a yard swing in Ohio.

4

And everything rises that is at first unsaid.
Signs return to the emptiness

of a shouldered line, the forest where trees
separated from each movement, partway between

what is moved and what is transient in its movement.
There is no glory, but the understanding

of glory, as if it were a given fact of a sentence fated
to remain in the dark, part and parcel of the

tree line, weighted down, as if water surrounded
each vessel and gave limbs their proximity to night's

dislocation, discord's mnemonic register, captive
partitions buried deep in the body's memory.

In ancient language to return where we lay
'our shaggy limbs naked on the ground

like bristly boars and blanketed ourselves
with leaves and branches.' The river on fire

in the field before us, light, the constellated
light of the heavens, retrieved from sight

a band of light broken in our hands.

5

I traveled back to see you, gutted séance, a pact

clarified as much by what you didn't say as
by what you offered. The dark curving figure

that remains uppermost, if you had recovered
patience, become its answer, slow to change where

the night air became another piece of history. I
was waiting, the end of a lifetime that parted

company, settled the score between heaven
and a landscape carved from sandstone & basalt.

And to re-occur is to bless what was…

Nothing blossoms but the trees that rest in a line
of blossoms. The hands trace their simulacra

to reiterate where blossom might be, where tree
line recedes, winter giving way to storm clouds passing

over, cracked light of the heavens, opening, turning
the ground away from itself.

6

To reiterate phases of the night: simple to re-create
steps, journey through each window

'days that wax and wane as nights'
increase the distance between

each passing day, light foreshortened by what it
re-instructs, this imbalance, like a dance

moving over water, the sign that one is
separating from one's body, as if constriction

became the false presence
of a body separated from its housing

now renewing itself, now separating, dark pull
of the meat, bone, loose tendon the body

frees itself from...

7

And what can be seen is the distance night
reiterates: Lethe's strangers returning to their

positions below the surface that travelers
must cross again and again, as one is bent into the

coast of the moon's angle, moves through a partition
both Beloved and Unhealed.

What I took from you, what I valued is
this: a territory

I could make my own....a landscape
darkening lightening

within the folds of another
lifetime.

Shadow and scale......the errant
light flow of sound that passes

from *thee* to *thine*.

8

In this theater of language
to see the crossed equinox

flares floating above...

A tree in October, night dividing
still burning limbs

piece by piece, in color.

24 October 2018

CONVERGENCES: NEW SERIES
For Peter O'Leary

>   re-invoke, re-create
>   opal, onyx, obsidian
>
>   now scattered in the shards
>   men tread upon
>   H.D., *Tribute to the Angels*

1

Rising late to go out, sunlight up all across the
eastern skies, like paint applied to the side

of a boarded up structure, seen once in a shadow
dream, now far-off, ransomed, forgotten

in that place of body's late awareness, perception's
dream hold stiffening at the water's edge...

Was it vacated truth or reality's shadow
that informed our skin, torn at the joints, quiver

of rain, sight of the tree we said was one's house,
habitat of many nights. How understood

grief was, shared, virtual as one is made to stand
nightly at the window, corner lot, peer out

under Orion, not see what light there is, cast by
an old branch of light, scent's unequal

calendar. I was dreaming or kept to dream's
edge, a knife in place of sun, blades of color from creased

metal, like a surface of red water, weeded out
from light's stalling. There is this empyrean

shore, reddening, one says it's inside one's mind
to find it, settle beside it, lean into its chain

of referents, the way loose rock forms a gravely
slope at the river's edge. Can memory exact

fate in this way, damp, viscous, righted by mineral
skin from the low-lying cedar falls? What is

found, left over, the scat-born shot from inside
one's left ear, like a random recollection, seer

and object for a time joined.

2

One to one, we said, in some faith, faithless
was the same as shapeless, we said the days

were of little account, one came back from the
journey or didn't, Ithaca or Cairo, we had no

names for where we went, the days passing each
one like the other, no one like any other, blue

skies or red, the seasonal occupation as we read in
Ovid of a hill, surface that appears to the left

of us, the way this hill kept an open space, residual
level area, made green by grasses growing there.

And it was like one's arboretum from some absent
dream, sky and shore-like wind, the same to

come back to, level hill, surface area for trees
in a row, as if residence could be imagined at this

juncture of world-making, Aeolian shiver, river
of resounding sound that passed through the world...

A grove of poplars (once Heliades) and the Italian
oak, with its grooved deep green leaves, the first

linden, beech and laurel, unwed, breaking inside a
rim of color, cotton beside laurel, ash that had

been gifted for spears and javelins, in name only
falling to the ground, beside the acorn-laden ilex.

And the grey falcon passing above canonical red light....

3

Did we take the black
tree, one to one in gods'

rift, a sign from one
world to another? Said

it was travel made us move
again, berries on the

vine, we said here are
black and green ones

to find. Recognition's
finger that points daily

to otherness inside our
claim, of bodies lifted

to rest, residual, risible
stations. In passing, as one

leans toward Cybele, her
beloved Attis put aside

his manhood for that trunk
blackening in a low

spring frost.

4

At every stage, the articulate
waters, red-leafed, bent

wire from childhood insecure
as leaf-blown

ash, one ventures near the end-point
to come back inside

ragged root, housed
by a range of birds

overlooking the sea
bending their call to no one....

5

A new sensation
is not granted to everyone...

As the border between this world and the next
forms a lexical divide, arcana's wisdom, the loose

foil that secures wood beams together in a windstorm.
We're carrying ourselves nightly into the woods

to witness the light decrease, as someone said to us
once, the wideness of the world is viewable as a line of

poetry, the self is removed from itself, one says there is
plenty, food inside the shelter that stands halfway

between here and wherever. Some sun, the granules
of light, easterly wind, so everything softens, as thematic

content is cleared away, building and forest become two
alignments the body moves toward. I was waiting

for the light to change, east by southeast, to turn
away from its providential mastery. Another's words

could turn me in time, turn the self into a kind of soil
reworked, the body of oneself reworked, soil as the loan

one's body partook of and shook itself to receive. My body
at the water's edge, forest where there was one limb crossing

a meadow, the permission of one passing from here to there
in soil time, the record exact and loose as sumac

bending into a westerly breeze.

6

And depth is formed from particulars
that sight can allay, decrease, like wind through

an open window, March light, the entry point
of yesterday, an hour earlier, to house oneself

in light, skin is a frame, born from its wafer
to comb the earth again, light from outside

oneself, as Olson made his house at Watch
Point, to refuse delegation, sure as his hand

was the scent was real, eternal, world o
world of light and water, sea's green from

enchanted dream...

7

Yet to walk again is to create the context
for walking, as one remembers names for the

earth flowers they see *nelumbo lutea
nymphaea advena troillus laxus*

*actaea rubra micranthes saxifrage penthorum
sedoides* each conjecture

Latinate color and sound, rime of each
season, to see and say, one is making sound

to see and say, the locality of one's habitude that
is always already in view, as if stationery

one had lost sight but gained ground, regained
hearing but lost sight, this emblematic

tag world, provisional, polychromatic
as if music had set up ladders

and made us invisible.

8

The record of any day is this estrangement from
all days....one is living inside or the outer

rim of water hasn't reached the surface, color
of a river view from this distance, as if all

effort were this plurality, this vocal beseeching from
another life. We were keeping to the body of

Ohio, the waters had resumed their course, every
hour came back as re-lived paternity, patient, singly

put, one is leaving the channel, a river house
slips past, we're in company of its movement

as any life is less and less real than what is provided
it by way of shelter, movement, the crossing

it makes at night. Sojourning southwest at morning
to see the light move across the Ohio river valley

as one is returned to first forms, to light and silver
patches, a record inside one's pocket, the lifted

heliocentric portrait of a river, sandstone, buildings...

9

Pages of a book fall....not less than any
other, no less real than this

passing of pages, offered for
light, small prayer, the lines of another

crossing over our own...

There is one law of averages, another
of sundial mornings, skin raw from the wind

yesterday, taking myself back outside, rays
of light, as if recollecting what it was

to inhere, stray motes, skin's ample
conjecture, conjunction of 'o' and 'a'

sympathetic shade, sullen bird
song, to recall its ambient sly

movement, as I'd read in Thoreau's
journals once, 'the song sparrows are very

abundant peopling each bush-willow or alder
for ¼ of a mile & pursuing each other

as if now selecting their mates' (Mar 16th 1864).

10

At rest with no one, but sky's
heavy foil, rain imminent...yesterday's

skies darkening, less realistic, though no less
dominant, saw myself go into their

layers, bracketed sorrel and chestnut
cut from memory, a kindred spirit

passing by, one says shelter, another seizes
on the opportunity of silence.

What did I dream of there, by your
side that now I can't recall the color of sky

or if rain fell or the ground became
sodden and heavy with rainfall. Sunrise is less able

to come when the light goes, sere yellow,
dark orange at the poles between

there & then.

9 March 2021

THE VIRTUAL SON

> I will walk up and down here,
> And I will walk up and down here,
> And I will sing.
> Louis Zukofsky, "[A-12]"

1

In late afternoon
the light convinces

us of this place
expansiveness of *this* late

afternoon light
held in common

sun light that seems
to part company with earth.

Sun and shade
interstitial phases

parting company
with earth.

We have these few
things

were given these
few things

afternoon sun
that comes through

a millionth of a second
in time the sun light

coming through
a millisecond of light

moving through a quadrant
coequal with landscape

light that falls across
a pattern of hills

slow time of hills and light
moving solitary and in time

these principle
acts of our bodies

watched from inside this body
of light that falls

across the western hills
blue ovals slipping into black

your voice purgatorial
across the years this triangulation

of bodies carved from light.

2

To see the earth inside
in the open

situate the eye
as care for its objects

not one but two
coming into contact

not one but two
moving through a scene

Landscape
as charge and habitude

to see it is to say
what isn't here

an absence held
private written apart from saying.

3

When on the borders of the land

a farmer working the earth
opens the ground again.

A threshold
the landscape is a threshold

one says they will come back to it

the man is in the field
white stones across the yellow

lines of light
the falcon come back for sparrows

survey what is coming
in light the shade of water

across the field his heavy hoes
beat on hollow helmets

become old against all odds
the sleeve will open out

border of red grass
sleep will come back

to haunt
the frame uprooted

from its center
this polity of light

balanced near the end time.

4

What was the instrument delivered us to you....

What can be known
can't be quantified

There is this journey
we were told it would come

from inside the young
days lightened by not speaking

but care when it came
incapable of another's

embrace
or language—

act as if together
were one

all things inside
the light were within

one's grasp
a sayable world

brought back in
conception's flowers

late-blooming philox
in a pot bending into

southeasterly light.

5

'Looking up I envy the evening birds,
lodging in forests, their wings so light.'

Each of us can imagine
no day apart from other days.

Company of the separate
spaces we inhabit.

The birds move without voice
or volition but remain part of what I

imagine when I turn away, their
flight that occurs without return.

One, two, three
the days are following

patterns, only the image
of a voice

opening, warmth
of light on skin

the sun moving
down field in bands of red.

Dream-work of the ordinary.
The curtains inside a frame.

How do I renew what is
related, resistant, a band of

sparrows crossing through
spare heaven. I have returned too

late to reappear here. The daylight
orphaned by our bodies, a systemic

re-working of the self that is without
trace of having been. Here inside

the darker days, a separation
that is also companionate, as if to return

to one's hands, know one's hands
can shape what's returned to them.

To know the work lifted from us
through the night, like Du Fu's

bamboo that cooled his eyes
so he could remain in one place.

Revisiting the room where he slept
I settle as he did into the scarred

memory of fireflies staying the night
on the water, the birds calling to

each other, a vision of earth's yield.

6

Nostos wind
at mid-day

the disinheritance
of a woman's voice

empties into mine
not used to speaking

the voice co-opted
inside a principle of saying

comes toward me
light from the trees where light

has comes to rest

Light resolves itself near
boxwood green

See the fields
shape themselves in light

tree from tree
the birth of such things in locality

as pine offers wood to carpenters
cedar and cypresses for houses

one by one they enter
the open

to build their homes at the river's edge
open themselves again to light

taking the shape of such objects
encirclements

come into one's hands
take on the shape

of tools
hollowed out with a point of iron

as the supple alder swims
through twister waves

speeding down the Po
and bees conceal themselves

in holm oaks
buried light from the forest.

7

What distresses
the system to distress

a system in light
care for its parts

as bodies are gathered
in a field of white flowers

To move as memory dictates
difficult to enter the scene again

a system of names
cingquefoil

yellow and green
stems ascending a few

inches high
yellow light heightened in mid-

summer
the ground spread

by slender runners
to become aware of each movement

petioled leaves
digitally five-foliated   their leaflets

oblanceolate to oblong
the first flower appears without

yellow
blend of green and blue

the flower

separating from yellow is turned
without light to the ground

on which it turns
a base of yellow

river light when the flower
turns away from us

whitening
along a red branch

twilight the slender
summer light

suspended in a network of
calyx lobes and the linear

lanceolate braclets
stamens about twenty.

10-14 January, 2020

Coda

The embrace of the
Beloved

apart from light
becomes witness to

ourselves
apart from the Beloved.

Incapable of conspiring
together my hands are raised

not toward words but common
axioms of faith

belonging to no movement
I can define.

The river I remember is miles
distant as is the hawk that travels

each day above.

I am re-visiting their movements
throughout my days.

Among summer's late yellow
flowers I rest

without company at
daylight's end

as a circle of sunlight
is drawn around

my body.

The silver drum of cinquefoil
white crown of leaflets

poured down on rock's
hard surface.

Heaven above is never
one-sided.

Ascending
small yellow flowers

opening out
breaking from the heat.

Yellow cables of sun
demarcating a world.

10-14 January 2020-28 December 2024

Notes & Acknowledgments

A partial listing of the writers and texts that served as sources for some of the language and references included in these poems would include the following:

Elfriede Abbe. *The Plants of Virgil's Georgics*. Ithaca, NY: Cornell University Press, 1965.

Hannah Arendt. *The Human Condition*. Second Edition. Chicago: University of Chicago Press, 1998.

William Blake. *The Complete Poetry & Prose of William Blake*. Edited by David V. Erdman. New York: Doubleday, 1988.

Robin Blaser. *The Holy Forest*. Toronto: Coach House Press, 1993.

Aime Césaire. *The Collected Poetry*. Translated with an introduction by Clayton Eshleman and Annette Smith. Berkeley, CA: The University of California Press, 1983.

Robert Duncan. *The H.D. Book*. Berkeley: University of California Press, 2011.

Rachel Blau DuPlessis. *Drafts 1-38, Toll*. Middletown, CT: Wesleyan University Press, 2001.

Du Fu. *The Poetry of Du Fu*. Translated and edited by Stephen Owen. Boston and Berlin: Walter de Gruyter Inc., 2016.

Díwán of Háfiz. *Wine & Prayer: Eighty Ghazals from the Díwán of Háfiz*. Translated by Elizabeth T. Gray, Jr. and Iraj Anvar. Ashland, Oregon: White Cloud Press, 2019.

Han-shan. *Cold Mountain*. Translated by Burton Watson. New York: Columbia University Press, 1970.

H.D. *Trilogy*. New York: New Directions Books, 1973.

Jane Harrison. *Themis: A Study in the Social Origins of Greek Religion*. New York: World Publishing Co., 1969.

Kokinshū: A Collection of Poems Ancient and Modern. Translated by Laurel Rasplica Rodd with Mary Catherine Henkenius. Boston: Cheng and Tsui Company, 1996.

Denise Levertov. *Poems 1960-1967*. New York: New Directions Books, 1967.

Li Po. *The Selected Poems*. Translated by David Hinton. New York: New Directions Books, 1996.

Nathaniel Mackey. *Blue Fasa*. New York: New Directions Books, 2015.

---. *Splay Anthem*. New York: New Directions Books, 2002.

Ezra Pound. *The Pisan Cantos*. Edited by Richard Sieburth. New York: New Directions Books, 2003.

Ed Roberson. *To See the Earth Before the End of the World*. Middletown, CT: Wesleyan University Press, 2010.

Victor Serge. *Inhuman Land: Searching for the Truth in Soviet Russia*. Translated by Antonia Lloyd-Jones. New York: New York Review of Books, 2018.

Richard B. Sewall. *The Life of Emily Dickinson*. New York: Farrar, Straus and Giroux, 1974.

Robert Farris Thompson, *Flash of the Spirit: African and & Afro-American Art & Philosophy*, Vintage Books, 1984.

Henry David Thoreau. *Journals*. Multiple volumes. Princeton: Princeton University Press, 1981.

Virgil. *Georgics*. Translated by David Ferry. New York: Farrar, Straus and Giroux, 2005.

Xavier Villaurrutia. *Nostalgia for Death*. Translated by Eliot Weinberger. Port Townsend, WA: Copper Canyon Press, 1992.

Walt Whitman. *Leaves of Grass*. With an introduction by John Hollander. New York: Library of America, 1992.

Louis Zukofksy. *Complete Short Poetry*. Baltimore and London: The Johns Hopkins University Press, 1991.

*

"Mourning: A Work Song" appeared in *Conjunctions 82: Works & Days*. "The New Spirit" appeared in *Conjunctions 79: Onword*.

"The Separation of Earthly Objects'" appeared in *Conjunctions Online*, January 25, 2023.

"Parallel Suites for the Re-Recognition of Innate Form" appeared in a somewhat different version in *Colorado Review*, Summer 2021.

Many thanks to Bradford Morrow and Stephanie G'Schwind the respective editors of these publications, for their support of this work.

*

Thanks to David Need who read portions of this work in manuscript form and provided useful commentary that was incorporated into the revision of this book.

Much gratitude to Peter O'Leary, one of my earliest and most careful readers of my poetry. I am indebted to him for numerous suggestions that have made this book stronger across its pages, not least of which was a change to the title that brought forward Arendt's conceptual mapping into a more pluralistic form.

To Donald Revell I extend my deepest gratitude for his agreeing to read this manuscript in an earlier form and provide the comments that appear on the back jacket of this book.

Heartfelt thanks to Patrick Pritchett who read the book at a late stage in its writing and made vital suggestions for revision that have been incorporated into the final form of this collection.

A special thank you to Joseph Donahue for his support of my work across the many years of our friendship. His insights, shared knowledge and proffered "gifts" of materials and artworks have provided indispensable resources for my own work in poetry and have led me to look in directions I otherwise wouldn't have. Among those directions is the 19th century American painter, Arthur Wesley Dow, whose work is featured on the cover of this book.

To Tod Thilleman, I am grateful beyond words for his friendship, vision and insights into poesis and poetry in all their variant forms. As editor and publisher of Spuyten Duyvil Press, he helped me create through the numerous book projects of mine on which we've collaborated the singular path that made *A Common World* possible as the book it has become. For all our past, current, and future collaborations, I remain profoundly grateful.

For bringing *A Common World* into the world as a complete book, my deepest thanks to Eliot Cardinaux and all the folks at Bodily Press. Their singular efforts and positive energies make projects such as this possible in these increasingly uncertain times for poetries, their publics, and independent small press publishing in the U.S.

To my wife, Monica Jacobe, I owe a debt of gratitude for her editorial acumen, intellectual rigor, and insights that make every book I write better for her having read it first. This book would not have been possible without her wisdom, patience, and love.

About the Author

ANDREW MOSSIN is a scholar, poet and memoirist, who has published over ten books of poetry, including most recently *Black Trees* (Spuyten Duyvil); a collection of critical essays, *Male Subjectivity and Poetic Form in "New American" Poetry* (Palgrave); and a memoir, *A Son from the Mountains* (Spuyten Duyvil). He has most recently edited a collection of scholarly essays, *Thinking with the Poem: Essays on the Poetry and Poetics of Rachel Blau DuPlessis* (University of New Mexico Press, 2024). He is currently collaborating with Monica F. Jacobe on a book-length study of the photographer, visual artist, and sculptor William Christenberry. He is an Associate Professor of Instruction in the Intellectual Heritage Program at Temple University in Philadelphia.

THE BODILY PRESS
www.bodilypress.com